A LEGACY OF FAITH

WORDS FOR THE JOURNEY

ACROSTIC – noun. A poem, word puzzle or other composition in which certain letters in each line form a word or words.

A LEGACY OF FAITH

WORDS FOR THE JOURNEY

By

B.C.W.

Barbara C. Weathers

God bless you Bethany ♡

Revelation 2:10

2 Timothy 3:16

Redhawk Publications
Catawba Valley Community College
2550 US Hwy 70 SE
Hickory NC 28602

INDEX

Prose and Poems

DEDICATION

To my loving Husband of 49 years

Carroll Wayland Weathers, Jr.

To our First Born,

Carroll Wayland Weathers III

To my dear friend and accomplished artist and sculptor,

Norma Suddreth
For her illustrations

ACKNOWLEDGMENTS

This book is first and foremost a Tribute to

Jesus

Who is its actual author.

I am deeply grateful to the people whose computer management and Organizational skills created the content between these covers and to my precious Christian Saints

Arlyn Cherney
and
Sandy Dunbar.

Thanks to

Ann Lauterbach

Who consistently encouraged me and offered meaningful feedback.

"SIMON PETER ANSWERED HIM, "LORD, TO WHOM SHALL WE GO? YOU HAVE WORDS OF ETERNAL LIFE." JOHN 6:68

As one who has loved, studied and tried to obey the Word of God for seven decades, Barbara Weathers shares fresh insights into timeless truths from sacred scripture though acrostics. Each letter, placed vertically (forming one or two words), contains a Biblically inspired phrase, thus expanding the depth of the word used. Jesus said, "Heaven and earth shall pass away, but My Word shall not pass away." Matthew 24:35 Let these acrostics simply sink into your soul as you sit quietly under the guidance of the Holy Spirit. Engaging your mind and heart through these "Words for the Journey" will refresh your soul, grant renewed hope and motivate you to "leave a legacy" rich in faith.

Looking TO and FOR JESUS!

—Sandy Dunbar

FOR OVER FIFTY YEARS

Barbara and I have been close friends and have confidentially shared many of our life concerns and fervently prayed over them; but it was only recently in her humble and unassuming manner that she disclosed that during those years, she has written acrostics to the glory of God. These poems of praise have been mostly personal and only through the encouragement of others has she agreed to share them in this book.

In our world today of technology, we have lost many of the art formats we've enjoyed in the past. Literary prestige often has vanished. Barbara has restored to us, in her chosen method of using acrostic poetry, a form of communication used thousands of years ago in the Hebrew Psalms. Biblical study, education, musical background, and enthusiasm are all evident in the artistic skills she used to communicate a heart lifted up in worship to a God and Savior she knows intimately with devout affection that carries a holy warmth.

We should not just read Barbara's Spirit-filled and passionate acrostic poems, but use them as encouraging devotions of prayers, songs, praises, and most of all, worship to a God who is worthy

.—Eugenia Welch

I HAVE KNOWN
BARBARA C. WEATHERS

for most of my adult lifetime: as members of St Luke's Methodist Church, sisters in the homecoming of our sons who are now with the Lord, and now patrons of Safe Harbor Rescue Mission. In her Words for the Journey, Barbara speaks with a rhythm that all of us can hear. She brings God's Word to life with this publication of her acrostics. Like her love of music, her acrostic "poetry" sings of a faith that is authentic and genuinely touched by the hand of God.

—Patricia A. Anderson

IN MALACHI 3:16 IT SAYS THAT "A SCROLL OF REMEMBRANCE WAS WRITTEN IN HIS PRESENCE CONCERNING THOSE WHO FEAR THE LORD AND HONORED HIS NAME."

Barbara's main purpose for writing her book is to honor God's name. This book is a labor of love. Barbara receives much joy from writing and creating acrostics, and she values how much they glorify God. She would love to share her delight with you so that you, too, might experience this joy.

This is a book written by a pilgrim for other pilgrims who desire to take a spiritual journey with words. Barbara is a lover of God's word and these acrostics express that so clearly. Acrostics are a poetic tool to enable you to remember and apply the wonder of God's word. Hopefully, they will help you to grow and delight more and more in God's word. It's Barbara's desire that this will happen as you reflect upon her simple yet profound acrostic creations.

—Timothy and Anita Boyd

ABIDE

Abide always in Christ

Believing HIM with steadfast faith

In life and in death abide with ME

Drinking at the well of salvation that never runs dry

Enter now into eternal rest and enjoy God at HIS very best

John 15:4-11

ADORE

Adore Him forever more

Down to earth He came to reign

Overall, in all and through all He rules

Righteous Savior, Son of God, receive Him this day

Emmanuel, God with us, our precious
    LORD of LORDS and KING of KINGS

Song of Solomon 1:4

ADVERSITY

Adversity is a time of affliction, but a tool God uses to
    strengthen our faith in areas of greatest need

Distresses and disasters are universal and impartial
    tools to chisel us into shape

Very painful, intense and prolonged, but we are not alone,
    for God promises never to leave us

Every aspect of life will experience some form
    of adversity in this fallen world where we now live

Remember, God doesn't allow adversity to hurt us,
    but to help us make room for God to be
    exalted in first place

Sovereign power of the LORD allows adverse circumstances
    as His gift to change our wrongs for His ultimate glory

Intense agape love eliminates our excuses and
    causes us to examine our hearts thoroughly

Tragedies can be transformed into beautiful building blocks

Yield, bend, bow low before the changeless,
    perfect Father-God who cares for you and
    loves you unconditionally

Proverbs 17:17

ARMS

Available always

Remarkable are His arms

Mighty in power and strength

Secure and warm

Deuteronomy 33:27
Isaiah 51:5

AUTHORITY

Actually, all authority stems from Christ Jesus

Underneath Him we have divine protection and security

This is truly

Holy truth

Offered to guide and lead us into a right standing with God

Relationships show reverent respect and honor to God's ruling authority

In Christ who is above all, in all and through all

Trust and obey to please God

You will be blessed and have eternal rest, so thanks be to Him forever and ever

Amen

AWESOME

Awesome God

Wonderful Savior

Everlasting Father

Shepherd

Offers His grace, loving kindness and a new life

Mighty Counselor

Everything we ever have need of is found in HIM

BEHOLD

Behold the man and see

Everlasting Father God dying for you and me

Holy Jehovah, Mighty God

Our Price of Peace, just and righteous in all His ways

Lord of Lords and King of Kings, our sacrificial Lamb of God

Divine Redeemer, our risen Savior, gaze on Him who has no
     equal

Matthew 28:16
Hebrews 10:14

BE VIGILANT

Be faithful, fully committed

Eternally thankful to the living God

Vigilantly guard your soul

Interested in pleasing HIM above all else

Great is HIS holy covenant

In humility we vow to never forsake HIM

Leaving no stone unturned in loving behavior

As we strive to remain obedient to HIS will for us

No good thing will HE withhold to those who live uprightly

Thanks be to HIM forever and ever
                    Amen

Deuteronomy 22:1-6: Chapter 24
Joshua 23:1-11

BOLD

Boldness to please Jesus alone

Offers opportunities while

Listening to hear and obey

Divine directions for the day

Proverbs 28:1

BRING

Bring your silver and your gold, not a mite would you with hold

Remember to also bring your sacrifices of praise,

Inspired and motivated in heart to lay at His feet every thought, motive, purpose or deed

Nourished in commitment and fruit-bearing living

Going forward and growing in His loving grace

BROKEN

Brokenness of spirit in true contrition

Results in restoration

Offering real life and purpose for living

Knowledge of the Lord grows and matures

Energizing and revitalizing

Newness of life and zealous love in Jesus name

Psalm 51:17

CHILDREN

Christ's gift to us

Hearts HE touches in awesome ways

Interested in protecting and leading "the way"

Loving us perfectly everyday

Divine wisdom HE imparts

Reason to listen and obey, for there's no
     other WAY to be happy in Jesus

Everlasting arms of comforting love

Never is HE too busy to hear, for HE's
     always near my dear

                  Love, Jesus

Luke 18:16

CHRIST

Christ, our Lord and Savior, completely
    all we ever will need, enough

He must have preeminence in all things,
    so we can avoid deceptive entrapments,
    false teachers and their doctrines claiming
    fullness and freedom by formulas, - -
    minus devotion to Christ alone

Rescuer from the dark domain, Redeemer through
    His shed blood on the cross for us and
    raised us with Christ

Image of the invisible God in Heaven and on earth;
    we are made in His image and our life is
    hidden with Christ in God

Sons of God, Emmanuel, God in the flesh with us,
    controlled by the Spirit to teach us His truths
    through His WORD

The only way, the only truth and the only real life;
    thanks be to Him, our faithful, grace-giving
    Father God, Divine Redeemer – Holy Jesus

      Amen and Amen

Colossians Chapters 1-4

CHRISTMAS

Christmas Christ, God with us

Holy Prince of Peace

Risen Christ, sacrificial Lamb of God

I AM who is and was and ever shall be

Savior, Divine Redeemer

The Everlasting Father, King of Kings and
    Lord of Lords

Mighty God

Amazing is He, full of loving grace and truth

Strong, wonderful counselor, our greatest
    Christmas gift; our perfect guiding Light

John 1:1-8

CLING

Cling to Him

Live in Him

In your daily walk actively reflect the
      brightness of HIS glory

Never too busy to offer a cup of cold water
      in HIS NAME

Giving and sharing always the love of Christ
      and your reason for such joy

Colossians 2:6

CLING II

Cling to HIM with a firm, confident grip

Leaving behind all doubts and fears

In faith stand, believing you will see HIS promises fulfilled

Never ignore warnings from prophets or God's Holy Word
    delivered to you via the HOLY SPIRIT

Grow and become more genuine as one of HIS own
    bringing salt and light into this fallen world

COME

Come, commit fully

Offer yourself wholly to Jesus

Move over and let God move in

Experience the nearness of the living God
as He enfolds you

1 Samuel 7:3

COME HOME

Come home and praise the Lord

On bended Knee to meet God face to face

Meekly and humbly follow him

Each step of your way, all the way every day

Psalm 95
Psalm 150

COMMIT

Commit your ways to the Lord

Ordered by the Lord are steps of a good man

Much joy and delight await those who wait on the Lord

Mercy and peace fill one's heart with patient love

Increasing a desire to know Him better each day

Trust in Him, not in man, for He is the great I AM

Psalm 37
Psalm 118:8

COMPASSION

Compassion is consciousness of others distresses

One to another showing HIS everlasting kindness

Merciful concern will bring consolation

Pity shows compassionate sorrow

And wishes to bring comfort and tender love to the hurting

Shows favor and a willingness to help

Sympathetic graciousness never fails

I AM is full of compassion and will guide you with care

Offering hope and peace

Nourishing every fiber of your heart

Psalm 103:13

COMPROMISE

Compromise is not a Godly option

Only God's revealed way works best

Mindful of God's will, Jesus

Provides a path of eternal security and protective peace

Rest in the Lord and wait patiently for His directions

Only God knows the end from the beginning

Misery and missing the mark, results in trying to
mix good with evil

Insisting on "my way or the highway" leads to disaster

Serve the Lord and HIS precepts

Examine your heart honestly, be single-minded in
purpose, and don't lose sight of the prize of the high
calling

Psalm 143:10

CONTINUE

Continue to believe and trust in Jesus

Ongoing determination to put Him first

No turning back

Toward His way and truth

In growth and wisdom

Never forget who you are in Christ

Unending love, joy, and peace is available

Eternally supplied through the power of the Holy Spirit

John 15:1-12
2 Peter 1;4
John 17;17
John 8:31

COVENANT

Covenant, a legal binding promise

Offered throughout all generations

Verified, confirmed from Abraham to Isaac to Jacob

Everlasting possession it is

Noah was promised by God to never destroy the whole
earth by flood

An established "first" between God and Abraham

Never to be forgotten that God's blessings are eternal

Throughout history, God keeps His covenant

Psalm 105:8-10

DELIVERER I

Delivering Lord, my trustworthy buckler

Equips us when we submit to Him

Lovingly I will sing His praises

In my brokenness, He hears and delivers, when I cry to Him

Victory is on the way

Enlightenment breaks through my darkness

Remembering, without Him I can do nothing

Enabling me to trust and wait faithfully

Resting in God's total perfectness, He rescues the weary

Psalm 18

DELIVERER II

Depart from evil, for the Lord will hear your cries

Encamping around you are God's angels

Love, magnify, fear and bless the Lord at all times

In coming with a broken heart, and a contrite spirit, the Lord will save, protect and come close to you

Victorious you will be saved and delivered

Enjoying His blessings as you have tasted and seen He is very good always

Rejoice and give thanks forevermore, realizing He's your strong deliverer

Psalm 34

DILIGENCE

Diligence is to

Incessantly learn perseverance in all circumstances while

Leaning on His everlasting arms.

I choose to enroll in His class, so I can

Grow and mature in divine, purposeful living,

Earnestly prevailing in prayer which now becomes as

Natural as breathing to persevere with patience

Consistently, and with tenacity, as I seek to be more like Him each day in every way.

2 Peter 3:14;
1 Peter 1:5;
James 1:2-3 and 5:17

DOUBT

Don't camp on doubt ground

Our heavenly Father can be trusted-
   only believe

Unbelief is a serious sin dishonoring God

Boldly remember HE is the bread of life and the great I
   Am

Truly our Redeemer and our High Priest who intercedes
   in our behalf

Matthew 21:21

EASTER

Elohim, the only true God

All powerful Adonai

Saving Shepherd, our prince of peace

Triumphant King of Kings whom no grave can hold

El Shaddai, God Almighty, the Everlasting Father

Risen Lord with healing in His wings because of His
    resurrection love and power

1 Timothy 1:17

EMBRACE

Embrace things God permits into your life,
  for He is equipping you for new purposes

Make focusing on Jesus, and His truths,
  your daily reason for living

Boldly come to Him in prayer, because the veil has
  been rent, enabling a personal relationship

Rest in Him completely and rejoice always

As He has dealt with every circumstance you
  will ever encounter

Constant and perfect is our precious Lord

Expect every circumstance to ultimately be woven
  into a pattern of good that glorifies God in His time

Philippians 3:11-12
Galatians 6:9

ENCOURAGE

Encourage one another

Never neglect to do so

Caring love and compassion give

Offering hope to the hopeless

Underneath us are His arms

Reassuring us of His care

Aim to comfort willingly

Giving a word in season

Enables the hopeless to rest all cares, and trust Him totally

Deuteronomy 1:38

ENCOURAGER

Eager to encourage by example

Never negative

Constantly a comfort and counselor

Offers unlimited spiritual and physical resources

Unconditional love and support

Reassuring always and rejoices in your success

Anxious for our success, by
recognizing our abilities

Generously sacrifices

Enables you to achieve your full potential

Remains in the background when
accolades are passed out

ENDURE

Endure to the end

Never falling away

Do abide and stay

Until that great and notable day

Remain is to endure, so

Eternity is sure!

Matthew 24:13, 22,35
1 Corinthians 13:7
Ephesians 6:18

ENDURES

Endurance when all around seems visibly hopeless

Not relying on anything less than the invisible
power of God at work

Determined that nothing will shake my faith in Him

Understanding His character and perfect timing gives
hope

Resting in the Lord and waiting patiently because
of His enduring love

Enter now into a period of true worship and praise

Sees you through the storm and a secure landing,
and a right standing with God, which replaces
hopelessness with joy.

Hebrews 11:27
Psalm 37
Psalm 43:5

EQUIP

Equipping us by His blood for every good work He's as
    signed to us

Quick to be obedient in our relationships with each other to
    let us be

Undergirded with the covenant truth to do what is pleasing

In His sight, by His strength and

Power to depend on Him completely for the
    accomplishment

Hebrews 13:20-21

EXAMINE

Examine your heart diligently

X-ray type of search

Also see if there be any wicked ways therein

Make sure to confess after you are shown any errors

Illumine every corner as you inquire of HIM

Never leave the search incomplete

Enjoy then the freedom and peace that is surely to follow

Psalm 26:2
2 Corinthians 13:5
Jeremiah 17:10

FAITH I

Faith, not by feelings we must walk

Always faithful to Jesus, even when we're rejected
or misunderstood

Influenced by Him and not by the world

Trusting in His Word alone

Help me to pass the test of trusting even when His
presence is not felt

Hebrews 11:1-3, 6
Romans 1:17
Romans 5:1

FAITH II

Faith is dependence on God alone,
   minus any of our schemes

Aware of all our needs in every circumstance
   is our faithful Lord

I can, and will, praise Him at all times

Trust Him, for He makes no mistakes

He will deliver me and set my feet out of miry
   clay

Psalm 56
Psalm 34

FEAR I

Fear not for the I AM is with you

Ever ready to hear your concerns,

And calm your fears with HIS truths found in HIS WORD

Rest in the redeemer, and recall past times
    HE's delivered you from your troubles

Psalm 34:9-20
1 Peter 3:10-12

FEAR II

Fear is not from God

Early will I learn to lean on God

As vain imaginations can entrap and make
　a fearful mind

Remember two reasons not to fear-
　"I am your shield and your exceeding great reward"

Genesis 15:1
Proverbs 1:7
Isaiah 41:10-13

FEELINGS

Feelings are not reliable in making right choices

Each decision needs to be in line with God's WORD

Even when you don't feel like doing what God says,
do things His way

Leaning on Him, later you can be victorious

Invest time in prayer and obedience

Never will you regret trusting in His truths

Get over your hurt feelings and disappointments

So you can live beyond your feeling - a life without regrets

John 10:10

FOLLOW I

Fall on your knees

Offering your whole self

Laying down your agenda for His

Loving Him with all your soul, your might and strength

Onward pressing to that great and notable day of the Lord

Winning souls daily to follow Him forever

Matthew 4:19

FOLLOW II

Follow ME all the way

On the path I AM walking

Leaving old sinful behaviors behind

Leaning and pressing

Onward to the high calling in Christ Jesus

With renewed purpose of living in the
Spirit and not in the flesh

Matthew 4:19

FULLY

Fully obey and walk in His truth

Under no circumstances allow any partiality

Live without compromise

Live to glorify the Lord with your all

Yield to His every command

Ephesians 6:7
Colossians 3:17, 23

GLEAN

Glean in the field of His promises

Lean on His everlasting Love

Each burden He bears, strengthening you

Acknowledge Him totally in all circumstances

Now listen as HE softly and tenderly calls you to His precious
bleeding side to rest and trust Him totally

Ruth 2:2
Psalm 65
Proverbs 3:5-6

GLORY I

Gracious God

Loving

Omnipotent

Righteous Redeemer

Yahweh

Psalm 34:3

GLORY II

God's eternal perfect

Love that's rooted and grounded

Offered personally by Him

Resonating within your heart

Yearning to be strengthened and
　　empowered daily to glorify Him

Ephesians 3:16-17

GLORY III

Glory of the Lord shines where the Spirit of the Lord dwells

Like in a glass, we behold Him with an open face

Our Lord Jesus changes us from glory into glory

Removing darkness and giving light as we behold Him

Yahweh, our glorified Lord, to Him be all praise
forevermore

Amen

John 17:10
2 Corinthians 3:18
Isaiah 64:1-6
Psalm 115:1

GLORY IV

Glory power given to us now to strengthen us

Living life from the inside out, as you're looking
       to Jesus for all your needs

Opening us to a faith that believes, and loves
       to bless as we've been blessed

Remember I AM your Divine Redeemer

Yesterday, today and forever Amen

Ephesians 3:16-19
Hebrews 1:3

GLORY V

God of all glory thunders

Like the voice of many waters

Over all the fiery storms of life

Revealing His power and majesty

Yahweh gives strength and peace, as we
      give Him praise, glory and true worship

Psalm 29

GLORY VI

God's light to a dark world His glory

Love that's perfect in righteousness

Over and above lies

Radiant in His glorious splendor

Yesterday, today and forever. Amen

Psalm 57:5
Psalm 108:5
Luke 2:9

GLORY VII

God's glory is compatible with His character

Love like this endures forever

On display, filling places

Reflected on the faces of His people, the Shekinah
glory

Yielded and lived out to glorify Him forever, as
His grateful bondservants

2 Chronicles 7:1-10

GOSPEL I

Good News

Offered for

Sinners like me

Promising

Eternal

Life for the "whosoever will"

Prescription directions: Take "Gospills"
4 times each day

*Warning: do not skip a dose

GOSPEL II

Good news; the gospel is for sharing

Offered to whosoever will

So comfort one another, so

Prisoners can be set free

Eternally

Loving only Jesus, the Lord of their life

Mark 1:15
Philippians 2:5-11

GOSPEL III

Good news

Offers eternal hope

Sets us living for Jesus

Proclaims the only real truth

Everyone needs to know Him

Life from death blooms and raises a sweet
aroma in Father God's nostrils

John 3:16-18
John 17:3

GUARD

Guard your hearts continually

Understand the heart is desperately wicked
and Holy God knows all

Anchor yourself in God's WORD

Resist not His chastening; take responsibility
of these revealed truths

Do become more obedient daily for there is no
freedom without responsibility

Proverbs 4:23

GUARD THE FAITH

Guard your hearts, thus preserve your life

Understand the power of God's WORD

All I have commanded, do...go...tell

Rescue the perishing

Devote your life to glorifying your precious
Lord in every way possible.

Faith supports

And believes wholly

In the unswerving faithfulness of the Lord

The living Christ, Your Father God

Holy, perfect in all wisdom and truth

Psalm 91:1-4

GUIDE

Guide me daily precious Lord, and hold me with
YOUR powerful right hand,

Until I'm on the path YOU have chosen for me

Instill in me the will to yield

Determined to trust and obey

Embraced in YOUR grace and peacefully blessed with
eternal rest

Psalm 73:24

HALLOWED I

Hallowed be thy precious name

Almighty, holy God

Loving and perfect in all ways

Leaving nothing undone

Only doing what God says to do is the Jesus way

Without HIM we can truly do nothing

Everlasting Father

Divine, delivering Redeemer

Matthew 6:9

HALLOWED II

Hallowed be thy precious name

A mighty thirst and hunger for more bread of heaven

Longing to be in HIS arms

Languishing for more and more of HIM

Only HIM do I desire

Wholly do I lean on HIM

Everlasting Father, my divine Redeemer

Drinking at HIS well of salvation

Luke 11:2

HEAR

Hear to obey, to heed, God's WORD

Enthusiastic our willing hearts should be

Always keeping a teachable spirit

Ready to respond as He directs

Psalm 95:7-11
Ephesians 2:10

HEART

Heart is where God dwells and looks on us

Encouraging us to examine it thoroughly

A broken and contrite heart God will not despise

Righteousness reigns within a pure and clean heart

Take heart whole heartedly and guard it fiercely

Ezekiel 36:26

HELP I

Help is healing health from You, Almighty God

Embrace the power this help brings

Letting go of all hindrances that would block
　　the Holy Spirit's flow

Putting ourselves at total rest, so You can work
　　Your very best

Psalm 121

HELP II

Help comes only from the Lord who made all things

Every need is found in HIS eternal WORD

Leave all burdens at the foot of the cross with Jesus

Peace needs to be the umpire in all decisions, so there will be no regrets

Psalms 121:40,41

HOLY

Hallowed be thy precious name

On our knees, let our praises sing – Holy, Holy, Holy

Life flows in and through us because the
    Holy Spirit resides within

Ysuah, the Lord saves, and becomes our
    personal Abba Father

Isaiah 6:1-3
Roman 8:15
Revelation 4:8

HOPE I

Hope in the Lord

Only Jesus, who is my Savior, can give me this assurance

Provides me with a helmet of salvation to guard my mind

Expectation in Him gives divine hope

Isaiah 59:17

HOPE II

Hope in the Lord

Openly remember God is on His throne

Preparing perfect paths ahead

Enough tears now, for joy comes in the morning

Psalm 43
Psalm 30:5

HOPE III

Hope embraces resting faith

Opening one's hands into His perfect hands

Passing one's anxieties over to His patient care

Everlasting joy shall be yours, while knowing Father God
bears all your burdens

1 Peter 5:7

HUNGER

Hunger for His food, the bread of life

Until you are thoroughly satisfied

Nothing else but His Word can do

Grace and truth through Jesus

Endures forever and ever

Rest secure, realizing He is the Bread of Life

Matthew 4:4

JESUS

Jesus, just and true in all His ways

Everlasting Father, Immanuel

Savior, Guardian-Redeemer

Unfailing Lord of Lords

Sovereign God

Titus 2:13
Proverbs 8:8

JESUS THE LORD

Just and fair

Eternal God

Savior

Understanding love that knows us thoroughly

Same yesterday, today and forever

THE WAY, THE TRUTH, THE LIFE

Healer, helper, protector

Everlasting Father God

Lover

Of my soul

Redeemer

Divine and holy

Proverbs 1:3
Psalm 40:11
Mark 12:30

KINDNESS

King Jesus is full of loving kindness

Inviting us to practice kindness

Not a weak trait, but a Godly one

Divine provision for our needs shows
His kindness and love

Never will He forsake us

Eternal life we have in Him

Strongest defense we have, as we show
kindness towards others

Safe are we in His holy protection and presence

Psalm 32:10

KING

King, Priest Jesus, "Fairer than the children of men" (verse 2)

Is the center of Heaven's glory

No other can ever compare

God and man is He, King of Kings and Lord of Lords

Psalm 45

KINGDOM

Kingdom of our God and of His Christ

Is calling us to follow Him all the way

Now, immediately

Go forth proclaiming the gospel, the good news;
here you are led by the Holy Spirit

Delivering it in love, kindness and in truth

Offering your help in ways you are shown by the
indwelling Spirit of the living God

Making much of your opportunities to encourage
others to choose Jesus, the only true God,
King of Kings

Mark 1:15

KINSMAN

King of Kings

Israel's redeemer our redemption

Nothing is accomplished apart from His Word

Salvation from our enemies

Might was given, so we can serve him without fear

Always, and forever, the land of Israel I give to you

No other name given by which we are saved

Zechariah 4:6
1 Timothy 6:9-16

KNOW

Knowing God is being connected

Nothing can compare with this knowledge

Offers us wholeness in every sense of the word

Word of the Lord is power and strength to
overcome and become victorious

Psalm 115

LEGACY

Living now is a reflection of what we think of God

Every decision has an ultimate consequence

Great is our opportunity to be a walking example
  of God's love and grace

Aware of our calling, we are eager to bring
  Him much fruit

Create in me a heart fully devoted to the
  service of Jesus Christ

Yielded and molded by the POTTER'S HANDS – a life well
  lived for God's glory!

Exodus 28:29

LIGHT

Light came down when Emmanuel, God with us,
　　was born of virgin Mary

In Him we more and have our being,
　　our illuminator

God's glory shines so brightly we won't
　　need lamps in eternity

His light shines into all of our darkness:
　　past, present and future

Taking us into real life, as we walk in His light

John1:4-5
James 1:16-17
Revelation 22:5

LISTEN

Listen to hear God and to obey

In

Stillness and holy quiet will be your strength

Take God seriously; He means what He says and says what
     He means

Enlightened by His Word of truth and love

Now follow Him all the way

Mark 9:7
Proverbs 12:15

LIVE

Live Life

Invested in Jesus

Values and truths

Eternally secure in His Calvary shed blood

Ezekiel 16:6

LONGING

Longing for God, for without Him Life is meaningless

Only He can provide the true bread of life and living water that satisfies our real thirst

Nothing but the precious blood of Jesus can break our prison chains

Giving forth genuine stability and blessed assurance

Invest much time in HIS WORD and feast at His banquet table, for the banner over you is love

Now hope in the Lord and trust Him above all else

Great is His faithfulness and His mercies are new every morning

Psalm 42 & 43
Joel 1:20

LORD GOD

Leader

Over all, in all, through all

Righteous altogether

Divine

Greatly to be praised

Only perfect in all HIS ways

Directly involved in every aspect of our lives

Psalm 110:5

LOVE I

Love in Jesus takes away my bent to sinning

Over and around me are constant
    examples of His divine love

Vested interest in a personal relationship
    He has with me

Eternally to save and prepare a place in
    heaven that's secured by His grace

Psalm 136

LOVE II

Love is His commandment,
    His covenant and without it I am nothing,
    for His love is indispensable

Only Calvary love can wash away sins

Victory in Jesus' perfect love

Equals eternal life when confessed, repented and
    believed

Deuteronomy 6:5, 7:9
1 Corinthians 13:2,5

MAGNIFY IS TO GLORIFY

Magnifying the Lord

And bless His Holy Name

Glorify His

Name forever and ever

In everything let me stir up with thanksgiving remembrances

For all the blessings

You, precious Jesus, have provided for me

Psalm 69:30
2 Peter 3:1

MERCY I

Mercy and loving kindness

Encouraged and energized

Resulting in repentance and regeneration

Confidently trusting in Him

Yielded and fulfilled

Psalm 25:6
Micah 6:8

MERCY II

My mercy surrounds you, as God teaches you His Word

Ever present with you, equipping you for each new day

Readying you for the journey ahead

Circumstances are covered by His protective
    love, because the great I Am is always with you

Yahweh is the same yesterday, today and forevermore

Joshua 9:1-27
Psalm 23:6

MISSION

Missionary zeal has great appeal,

Inspired by love as gentle as a dove

Strong cords of faith lead one onward

So others can know HIS love too

In our desire to glorify God,

On HIM alone we must lean

Now out to the white fields to harvest and glean

Luke 10:2

OBEY

Obey Jesus every day in everyway

Because, in faith, there is no other way to

Enjoy life, endure hardships and receive God's best

Your walk in obedience will be redeemed on that great
    and notable day

OFFERINGS

One of many offerings we make to help spread the gospel

First fruits richly flow

Freely for His service here below as in heaven

Each day giving our best

Reminds us of His good grace

In all we do for His glory

Nothing will we withhold, so we can help draw others in the fold

Giving generously out of deep love we have in Christ

Sweeter than honey or the honeycomb is our privilege

Psalm 19
Isaiah 53:10

PASSIONATE COMPASSION

Compassion abounds in deep Calvary love

Offers consciousness of others distresses

Moves us with passion like Jesus

Perseveres and draws us to alleviate pain and bring
about comfort

Allows God to reveal needs as we are still before Him

Sensitive to His voice makes us

Sympathetic and full of wholehearted love in action

Invites relationships that encourage

Offering

New mercies that fail not under His Grace

PATIENCE

Patience requires much practice and prayer

Admit, confess this area of need to Jesus

Total willingness to work on this flaw puts divine
    help on track

Improvement in patience doesn't happen overnight

Expect your prayer for patience to be tested many times

Necessary to lean on God and learn
    new truths when you fail a test

Consistent practice, with determined focus, is a must

Enjoy the victory that will surely come

2 Timothy 4:12

PEACE I

Peace He gives, not as the world gives

Even in the midst of storms and troubles

Always He promises to never leave nor forsake us

Courage and boldness in Him removes fear

Expect God to uphold you with His mighty right hand,
            and you can confront fear head on

1 John 4:18
John 14:27 amp.

PEACE II

Prince of Peace, our personal Jesus

Everlasting Father, wonderful counselor

Ambassadors for Christ are we

Citizens of heaven are His faithful followers

Enduring the cross, He proved His perfect love, which is
eternally His finished work He was sent to do

Romans 5:1
Colossians 3:15
December 22, 2017

POWER

Power, love and a sound mind are gifts of the Holy Spirit

Only operative when plugged into the real source –
Jesus!

Watch out for burned out cords

Engage in a heart examination, so He can repair and
redirect your steps

Reset your electric panel box, so you can go forth
fully charged with His grace and power to lead a
purposeful, resurrected life for Jesus' sake.

2 Timothy 1:7
Ephesians 1:18-20
Philippians 4:6
James 4:6

PRAISE

Praise to the Lord, the Almighty, for He is
    our help and salvation

Risen Savior, righteous King of Kings

Amazing grace, mercy and loving kindness

Is found in Him

Sing to Him a new song, then

Everlasting joy shall be upon your heads

Psalm 149
Psalm 150

PRAYED

Prayed to the Lord who saves

Rested in Him alone who encouraged and rewards

Anxious not, but thankful

Yielded and still

Expecting perfect results

Delivered in His good time

Psalm 62

PRECIOUS I

Prefect and precious are YOU, Holy God

Resurrected

Eternal

Christ the Lord

Invisible and invincible

Only true God

Understanding Father of unworthy sinners

Savior, Divine Redeemer

1 Peter 1:19

PRECIOUS II

Precious and perfect is my Lord

Ready to hear our deepest cries

Everlasting and eternal love He gives

Christ my constant friend is He

In every circumstance He's near

Omnipresent, omniscient, omnipotent

Understanding, merciful and full of compassion

Secure I am in HIS mighty arms

Psalm 19
Proverbs 8:11

PRECIOUS III

Precious, prevailing, powerful, praying Lord Jesus Christ

Redeemer, resurrected, risen, reigning, righteous Lord Jesus

Everlasting, eternal, excellent Lord God Almighty

Carefully cherishing, cheering for us, constantly
      encouraging us

Invisible, inspiring, interceding Lord Jesus

Omnipotent, omniscient, omnipresent Lord

Understanding, uplifting, undeserved grace - giver

Steadfast Savior standing with us

Hebrews 1:3
Psalm 116:15
1 Peter 1:19

PRECIOUS LORD

Present in the now

Resurrection Easter power given

Eternal life poured out for all

Christ is the Risen Lord indeed—Hallelujah! Alleluia!

Immanuel now reigns with us

Opened paradise once and forever

Unending love abounds

Saving grace is ours to experience

Acts 3:17

PRIDE

Pride is a satanic heart-barrier

Removal of pride comes through confession to
    Jesus for forgiveness

Instruction gathered from an evil heart leads to

Destruction as a result of pride

Evil is from within, but can be removed at the foot of the
    cross

Proverbs 8:13
Proverbs 11:2, 11:7, 16:18
Matthew 11:24
John 9:39-41

PURITY

Purity is an imperative for us from Holy God
    for us to be HIS imitators

Understand that whatever is pure and praise worthy,
    we need to think on these

Resolve to resist the devil and flee from all
    fleshly and worldly desires

Truly those who are pure in heart are promised to see God

Yes and amen to all of the above

Titus 4:12

RECEIVE

Receive what you have in Christ with thanksgiving

Examine your heart in the light of His Word

Careful to check with God for His instructions

Every day with Jesus presents new opportunities
to serve Him

In all things keep God first

Victory comes by believing and receiving

Each morning the new mercies He brings; so
thanks be to God

Matthew 25:23
Psalm 16:11
Colossians 1:20

REDEEMER I

Rescuer, our Deliverer

Equal to no other

Divine Redeemer

Everlasting Father

Eternally our security

Messiah, our Passover Lamb

Egyptian bondage breaker

Ransomed and blood bought Savior

Mark 10:45
Hebrews 9:1

REDEEMER II

Restorer of life when

Every sin is confessed with Godly sorrow

Divine Redeemer is His name

Everlasting Father, the purifier of all evil

Elohim

Merciful and compassionate

Extravagant love He gives

Rescuing us with His healing peace

1 Peter 5:10
Isaiah 9:16

REFLECTORS

Reflectors of HIS glory

Each day we are given opportunities to do this

For

Light shines out of darkness

Everlasting joy radiates like Shekinah glory

Concentrating on the sharing of HIS WORD

To help turn others into light bearers too

Oh yes

Rejoice in HIM always

Seeing HIS undiminished glory we one day
will be changed from glory into glory

1 Corinthians 15:50-58

REFUGE

Rock and shield is He

Eternal God, a refuge in troubling times

Fortress, a mighty stronghold

Underneath us are His mighty arms

God is our refuge and strength

Ever near and equal to every need we have

Psalm 18:30-33
Psalm 46:31,22
Nahum 1:7

REJOICE I

Rejoice in the Lord always with all your heart

Even when you don't feel like it

Joyfully choose to adore HIM

Over you HE rejoices with singing

I AM will rescue and redeem you

Constant is HIS unconditional love for you

Eternal, everlasting praises to the mighty
    King of Kings, the great I AM

Philippians 4:4
Zephaniah 3:14; 17

REJOICE II

Rejoice in the Lord always

Every time the Spirit moves, rejoice and pray

Joy is a direct result of praising and
    rejoicing in the Lord

Offer prayer in all circumstances, for nothing
    is too hard for God

In the Lord, rejoice in HIS pardon, protection,
    precepts and promises

Constant praying, without ceasing, leads to
    peace that passes all understanding

Philippians 3:1
Zephaniah 3:14, 17

REJOICE III

Rejoice and sing; give thanks to the Lord our King

Exalted praises to HIM who equips us when we submit

Justice comes from HIS merciful hands at just the right time

O, sing praises for loving strength and protection

In everything give thanks

Covenants HE'S given never change

Eternally HE shall reign; hallowed be HIS NAME above all names

Psalm 18

REMAIN

Remain in me, so you can bear much fruit

Everyday remember to remain faithful
    to His WORD

Mindful of who He is, for He is all
    we ever need

Absolutely able to keep you rooted
    in the true vine

In HIM we have our ability to do for Him all He
    will ever ask of us

Nothing like this joy of serving Him can be compared

John 15:4-11

REMEMBER I

Remember it is the Lord who has made you

Eternal life HE offers to whosoever will

Make a joyful shout to the Lord

Enjoy all HE bought for you on the cross

Mercy HE spreads over our sins and
remembers them no more

Be thankful always and in all ways

Everyone is the same at the foot of the cross

Remember HIS holy covenant, and in adversity,
remember our response determines the outcome

Exodus 24:8

REMEMBER II

Remember the Lord your God who made you and
bore the curse of the law on the cross for you

Enjoy giving praise and singing of His wonderful acts
and the

Miracles and wonders He has done

Enter into His courts with thanksgiving

Mindful of His eternal covenant

Bless the Lord, and all that's within you, bless His
holy name

Established are His laws, for they are written on your
heart

Reassuring you that your confessed sins are
removed as far as east is from west

Galatians 3:10-13
Hebrews 8:12
Luke 1:68-73

REPENT

Repent, turn around, and return to the Lord

Every decision has consequences

Precious God wants restoration for sinners

Engaged, fully focused on His Word, teaches us eternal
purpose

Now is the day of salvation; I am waiting for you

Time to come back, for He longs to bless you

Isaiah 33: 1-6
Matthew 13:1-3, 4-17

REST

Rest means letting go and letting God run your life

Entirely trust Him who made you and
knows you thoroughly

Struggling is the opposite of resting

Trust God and let Him be Lord of your life

Proverbs 3:5-6
Psalm 37

RESTORE

Restorer of Life is our great God

Evermore interceding before His throne of grace for us

Seeking restoration following discipline to restore fellowship

True repentance needs forgiveness, acceptance and comfort

Offering peace and joy not as the world gives

Rejoicing over all the great things God has done

Eternally thankful and blessed by God who is the best

Psalm 126

RESTORER

Restore my whole being

Ever before me is my sin

Scrub and purge me 'til I'm white as snow

Truth and wisdom I desire above all else

O, God, make me joyful again and full of praise

Revive and renew a right spirit within

Even where sin abounded, Your mercy, grace
and love restores

Removing what the canker worm had eaten

Psalm 51

RESURRECTION

Resurrection of Jesus is proof of life after death

Everyone who embraces it has a reason
    to live for Him

Surrendering all to Him leads one to eternal life

Understanding His Word makes all things new

Raised to give us second birth while
    waiting for His reappearing

Risen with healing in His wings

Evidence of the empty tomb was proof positive

Calvary wounds are still in His hands

Triumphant Son of God

Is alive forevermore and because He lives, we can too

On the gospel rests the resurrection power

Now to Him all praise and glory as we joyfully witness
    His truths with zealous love and jealous
    care in all His children everywhere

John 11:25

REVELATION

Revealing, unveiling

Enthroned from on High

Voice of thunder shouting, "Time is nigh."

Enemy Vanquished forever

Lake of fire his home

Alleluia, Hallelujah

True believers enrolled

In the Lamb's book of life

Onward freely marching

Never looking back

Galatians 1:12
Luke 2:32

ROCK

Rock is cleft for me

On this solid Rock I'll stand

Christ, my resurrected Lord,

Knows my deepest needs and heart's desires

1 Corinthians 10:4
Solomon's Song of Songs 2:14

ROOTED

Rooted in Him, and in His Word, avails us of
strength of purpose in the midst of all
circumstances

On this solid rock we stand

Only by His Way can we produce fruit that brings
to God a sweet aroma

Trees of righteousness are steadfast and stable

Eternal security is a sure promise

Divinely planted in fertile soil of the heart that
leads to a life of grateful joy

Jeremiah 17:8

SACRED I

Sacred and hallowed is His Name

Anointed with total holy righteousness

Christ, the LORD

Redeemer, the everlasting Father

E Elyon, God most High

Dwells in hearts yielded and surrendered to
   this King of Kings, Jehovah

Matthew 7:6

SACRED II

Sacred, hallowed is His name

Anointed and totally Holy

Christ, the everlasting Father

Requires reverential fear as our source of wisdom

El, Elyon, God most High, nothing in life more sacred

Divine Redeemer, perfect in all His ways

Mark 1:24
1 Chronicles 16:10
Psalm 22:3
Psalm 77:13

SAVED

Son of God, given to whosoever believes in Him

An everlasting, nonperishable gift

Verily, verily I say to you, "You shall be with ME in paradise".

Extravagant, extensive, expensive, expansive
     is how God "so loved" us

Dimensional salvation was planned, provided
     and sealed by The Father, The Son, The Holy Spirit

Matthew 1:21
Hebrews 7:25

"You contribute nothing to your salvation except your sin that brought you."-Jonathan Edwards

SEARCH I

Search our hearts diligently

Examine them thoroughly

Actions, motives, and thoughts never deceive Holy
God

Realize we cannot escape, ignore or dispute YOUR
      knowledge of us

Carefully and intimately God knows us

His love is always perfect, for we were
      designed in His image to fulfill His plan for our lives

Psalm 139

SEARCH II

Seek Me while I may be found

Engage your whole self in this search

Attentiveness is key in finding ME

Relax, I am closer than your hands or feet

Call upon ME, and I will answer

Heart to heart I am giving MY love;
     calling to you in a variety of ways throughout
     each day

Psalm 139:23
Jeremiah 33:3

SHEPHERD I

Selected by God

His heart was one God loved

Every part of David's heart was after God

Picked, chosen, called

Herder of sheep was anointed and the Spirit
of the Lord was upon him

Endured many dangers, toils and fears

Respected, trusted and waited for God's timing of
his reign

David, the king God put on the throne in
the lineage of the Messiah

Psalm 23

SHEPHERD II

Shepherds His flock wisely and tenderly

Hears our bleating cries

Engaged in guiding and leading us into paths of
    righteousness

Preserves our ransomed souls

Heals broken-hearted lives, minds and relationships

Enduring love never runs out

Reigns in power to rescue and restore

Dutifully watches over HIS flock to defend us

Psalm 103:3
Micah 5:4
Psalm 23

SHIELD

Shielded, surrounded, protected on all sides

Help in Hebrew is to save

Is found in Jesus, our shield

Enlightens and comforts us

Lifts us above the circumstances

Defends and upholds us with His mighty right hand

Psalm 3

SIT

Sit patiently with me as I learn from Thee

I aspire in heart to let YOU lead me to that higher Rock

To obediently trust; stand up and faithfully walk to
the end holding on to the Victor's mighty right hand

"In the Garden" by C. Austin Miles, 1913

SOVEREIGNTY

Sovereignty of God characterizes the whole being of God

Overall, in all, through all is omnipotent God

Very God of Very God is He

Exercises HIS power when and where He wills

Ruler of all nations – the government is upon His shoulders

Exercises Sovereignty in His mercy and love

Incarnation of God's Son is one of the greatest events in the history of the universe

Grace gives God all the glory and extends the gift of Divine mercy to us sinners

Nothing is impossible with Him

The scriptures, God's Word, are absolute, irresistible and infinite

Yahweh – the same yesterday, today and forever

Daniel 7:27

STAND!

Stand up for Jesus in preparation for that
    great and notable day for

The trumpet call is not far away

Arm yourselves with gospel fervor as
    you dress for service with much prayer

Now rise above all battle noise to where
    our duty now employs.

Dare trust Him for strength and courage,
    for soon a crown of life will one day
    await those who don't fall away

STAND FIRM

Standing firm for the Gospel and its truths

Together with other believers

Arm in arm, united with one mind

Not only to believe in Him, but to suffer for Him

Dissuaded by nothing negative

Faith in God's gospel

Invites you to live worthy of your calling

Remembering suffering represents Christ and
strengthens enduring faith

Making us all better ambassadors

Philippians 1:27-30

STEADFAST

Steadfast is my trust under Your protective wings

Truth and mercy You send down

Exalted are You, my most high God

Adoni, LORD GOD alone

Deliverer, Emmanuel-God with us

Fixed is my heart's love for You

Always will I give You praise

Singing as I awake, and as You

Take me through the day and into night, for melodies
flood my heart, as I reach out and grasp Your hand

Psalm 57

STEADFASTNESS

Steadfast and constant in purpose

True badge of faith

Endures to the end with resolve and bold courage

Almighty God will keep you in perfect peace, when your mind is steadfastly trusting in Him

Dress in the full armor of God, so you can effectively stand your ground

Firmly fixed in place to face the race

Allow not Satan to ever attack your firm consistency

Strengthened and stable while remaining loyal and faithful

Truly as an ambassador to represent His Kingdom on earth as it is in Heaven

Acts 14:22
1 Peter 5: 6-10
Ephesians 6:11-18
"Courage is action in face of fear; be an overcomer!"

STRIVE

Strive to walk with God

To clothe yourself with HIS nature, for you
      are made in His image

Restrict, retire the flesh and let your
      strivings cease, so you can

Internalize His unconditional love and

Victoriously live with purpose

Everyday for Jesus as you try to
      please Him in all you do

Romans 8:29-30
1 Thessalonians 5:15-16

SUFFERING I

Suffering is never for no reason

Understand there are treasures to be
found in suffering

Focus on what God is trying to teach you
in the situation

Faith grows and deepens when you trust
Jesus in the situation

Exchange your "why me" for "why not me"

Remember "Who" is with you in the storms of life

Instructed by His Word is most important

Nothing escapes God's awareness of you

Give God praise and thanks in the storm

Romans 8:18

SUFFERING II

Suffering is a necessary refining tool

Under its challenges much gets examined

Faith removes masks that cover up root causes of the trials

Faith looks into the loving Father's face

Ever mindful that all He's doing is for our eternal glory

Remaking and redeeming us for Kingdom service

Instructing and inspiring us in how to press on to our calling

No complaining; just realizing God will see you through the trying tests

God will never leave you, for He is bringing His loving best faith through the refiners' fire

Romans 5:3
2 Timothy 2:3

SURRENDER

Softly and tenderly, Jesus is calling

Under His Spirit led power

Return unto ME on bended knee

Repentant and submissive

Eager to learn from Me

Never to withhold, so

Divinely He can unfold

Everything I need to hear

Resting in His best for me

Zechariah 1:3
Acts 3:19

THANKS

Thankfulness removes the sting of adverse situations

Hearts full of trusting and praising our covenant keeping
    God

Absolutely puts His joy deep into our souls

Nothing else can compare to this place of quiet peace He
    gives

Knowing that He inhabits the praises of His children

Sends His light shining on all our difficult paths

Philippians 4:7
Isaiah 30:15
1 Kings 19:12
Psalm 118

THIRST

Thirst for His living water

Hope in the Lord

Include Him first in all matters

Rest in the Lord always

Stand on His Word

Trust in the Lord with all your heart

John 7:38
Proverbs 3:5-6

TRANSFORMER

The Transforming Jesus in whom we believe

Rules and reigns in all of creation

All knowing and all powerful

Nothing beyond His reach

Sovereign God

Forever the same- THE GREAT I AM

Omnipotent

Reforms lost sinners

Makes all things new

Energizes our lives through and through - -
   minus disconnetions with the Source

Raises us up with resurrection power to be
   with Him in eternity

Ephesians 1:19-21
Romans 1:16, 15:13
Psalm 33:6-9

TRIALS

Trials are for testing and strengthening

Remember to count them all with joy

In the trying of your faith, much patience can be
    perfected

All hardships well endured shall receive the crown of life

Leaning totally on His everlasting arms

Secured and anchored to the Rock of ages, our safe
    harbor

Psalm 62:7-8
Psalm 107
James 1:2-4

TRUST I

Trust in Him who is tried and true

Reliable

Unbeatable

Sacred

Timeless

Hebrews 2:13

TRUST II

Trust in Jesus alone

Responsible thinking He gives

Undivided in purposeful living

Truth, pure and undefiled, He gives

Help and hope is ours for the asking

Proverbs 3:5-6

TRUST III

Trusting

Resting completely on Jesus'

Unconditional grace and loving kindnesses

Settling once and for all, to let go and let God

Take over and remake you fit for His service
     until He calls you home

Psalm 25:12
John 1:14-17
Jeremiah 5:1
Psalm 37:3-6

TRUST IV

Trust in the Lord with *all* your heart

Relying on Him, for

Underneath us are His everlasting arms

Satisfying our every need

Tried and forever true, precious Jesus

Proverbs 3:5-6

TRUTH I

Transparency

Repentance

Undefilement

Tried and examined by the Lord

Honesty and purity of heart He requires of us

Matthew 5:8
Psalm 51:10, 17

TRUTH II

Truth comes through Jesus

Receive truth through His Word

Understand who you are in Christ

Through His Calvary love

His Word is pure, unadulterated truth

John 1:17; 14:6; 17:17
2 John 3
Hebrews 10:1-4, 11-14

TRUTH III

Trust in the Lord with all your heart

Righteous living by walking in truth

Undivided focus is a force of undeniable reality

Testifying of the truth living in us

Holy and perfect to direct our work to glorify God

John 16:13
Isaiah 45:19
Proverbs 3:5-6

TRUTH IV

Truth is the total character of Jesus

Reliable and only source of life

Understandably the bedrock foundation
for everything that matters

Truth truly stands on its own merit

Honestly living to glorify Jesus who is The Way,
The Truth, The Life

Hebrews 13:18

TRUTH V

Truth is embodied in the I AM who is I AM

Righteousness is right standing in His truth

Unconditional love is His brand of truth

Trusting in His truth completely

Heals and seals your heart forever

John 14:6, 18:8
Exodus 3:14-15

TRUTH VI

Truth comes through Jesus

Receive truth through His Word

Understand who you are in Christ

Through His Calvary love

His Word is pure, unadulterated truth infused into your innermost being

John 1:17, 14:6, 17:7
2 John 3
Hebrews 10:1-4, 11-14

UNITY

Unity is a close relationship

Not to be casual, but

Inviting, progressive, deep and exciting

Timeless and sincerely earnest between

You and Jesus

Ephesians 4:3

VISION

Vision is more than 20/20

It grows in depth through the power of the Holy Spirit

Showing forth in many unexpected places

Increasing one's joy in the Lord

Openness to God's guiding light and His eternal view

Newfound truths found in the beauty of His Holiness
is true sight indeed

Joel 2:28
Psalm 19

VOICE

Voice of God is powerful

On day one He spoke, and it was

It speaks in thunder, wind and fire

Creation of God speaks of His sovereign glory

Every force of nature proves God is in control

Psalm 29

WAIT I

Wait on the Lord

Anticipate a new day coming

In perfect peace He will keep you

The Lord reigns, blessed be the Lord

Psalm 89

WAIT II

Willful impatience is not God's way

Anxious doubts must be prayed away

In earnest trust and resting faith

Turn all darkness into His light of day

Psalm 27:13-14

WAIT III

Wait expectantly on the Lord, no detours

Avoid the temptation to rush ahead of Him

Invest your waiting time in His Word and on your knees

Truths will be revealed and many mistakes avoided

Isaiah 30:18

WAIT IV

Wait on the Lord, for my hope is in Him alone

Are you able to remember who holds you in His arms?

Invest much time in His Word,
　　your Rock and Salvation

Then you will find strength and wisdom beyond
　　all measure

Psalms 62 and 39

WAIT V

Wait in prayer, in faith, in patient belief. He knows
   the real answer and the right time to give it

Anticipate HIS wisdom and perfect insightful knowledge
   in an attitude of faith

In God alone, you can have full joy, real protection
   and complete salvation

Trustful waiting on HIM, your strong tower of power,
   yields soulful rest in green pastures of hope

Psalm 27
Isaiah 51:5
Isaiah 64:4

WALK I

Walk with me dear Lord

As in service that's in sync with YOUR clear guiding
way

Loving kindness that strives through and through

Keenly motivating others too

("O Master let me walk with Thee" by Washington Gladden, 1879)

WALK II

Walk with me in YOUR light

Always

Leaving no shadow of doubt

Knowing YOUR WORD removes all darkness

Psalm 119:45

WHOLENESS

Wholeness is

Holy living

Offered to "outsiders"

Lovingly

Each new day

Not to be ignored

Embraced completely

Surrendered to

Sustained and supported as an "insider" with Christ-like
    living

1 Thessalonian 5:23
Matthew 6:22

WORD

Word of God is always trustworthy truth and applicable

Offering perfect answers to everything we ever have
   need of, so open and read

Reliable and full of wisdom to live by

Delivers truth without delay on His time table personally
   to you

Deuteronomy 8:3
1 Corinthians 2:13

WORDS

Words of the Lord are worthy to be leaned on,
    relied on and trusted

Offering power and reliable promises

Receive HIS word after hearing it with respect,
    love and obedience

Doers of the WORD – not just hearers only

Sharp sword of the Spirit is His Word; may we sincerely
    and wholeheartedly live it, so we
    glorify our Father who is in heaven

Psalm 119:42-56
2 Samuel 22:31
Revelation 2:26
James 1:22

WORTHY

Worthy of praise – to Him be all glory

Only One who is the I AM

Redeemer, our shield and our strength

The mighty God, the everlasting Father

Healer, helper – Holy is He

Yahweh, who is the same yesterday, today
and forever more

Amen

Psalm 18:1-3
Revelation 5:11

POETRY OF THE WORD

A BLESSING

For the Hand that feeds us and the heart that loves us

And the grace that forgives us,

Father, we thank Thee for these and all of our many blessings.

Amen

A MIRACLE ON EVERY CORNER

A miracle on every corner
Isn't uncustomary order
To God's born again creatures
Who've met the greatest of Teachers,
Jesus Christ – our blessed Savior!

BLESSED JESUS

Blessed Jesus, blessed Jesus,
How I adore Thee
Father, Son and Holy Ghost –
It is Thee I love the very most.

GLORIFYING HIS FATHER

Knowing HIS hour had come,
Jesus prepares for HIS return
Washing feet in humility, not defeat,
Exhorting disciples to practice this feat,
Thus loving as HE had loved.

Loving the unlovely, even a Judas,
So glorifying HIS FATHER to the end
May those we encounter know we've been with HIM
Not counting the cost, but taking up the cross
To follow, follow HIS risen end.

John 13

HOLY LOVE

All the way to Calvary for me
He willingly dies on that tree.
What holy love He shed that day,
So I could never lose my way.

Come one, come all!
Seek the Father, so you won't fall.
And learn from ME
Truths that will set you free.

HOLY SPIRIT, LIFE DIVINE

Holy Spirit, life divine,
To Whom there is the truth sublime;
Always guiding and providing
Strength and healing for revealing
Pearls of wisdom to Thy children
Who are starving and are thirsting
Until all within us is bursting
To know Thee, our only True
And loving God!

JESUS OPENS THE DOOR

Jesus goes before and opens the door

To provide for me what He has in store

To meet every need forevermore.

So daily thank Him more and more.

JOY AND LOVE REVEALED

Upon His countenance was Thy spirit of love and joy!
Oh how our souls rejoiced with this boy!
His heart too full to speak, but speak He did as You
Shone through laughing tears that glistened upon His
cheeks.

JUST AS I AM

Nothing can we bring
Only to the cross we cling
Come as you are
Follow the star
To be found not dead
But alive and fed
On His bread of life

Luke 15:11-24
Zephaniah 3:17

LIGHT OF THE WORLD

Light of the world, in Whom there is no darkness,
Thanks we give to Thee for relighting our candles this night.
May we ever keep them lit and above the bushel as
we step into Your world.

LOVE BLOOD

Oh my Jesus –
Every drop of YOUR blood was love blood
Poured out, spilling over, soaking through drop by drop –
Piercing every sin, thought, or act committed
Through the very marrow of YOUR being for me –
Such love from YOU
Soaks, cleanses, repurposes
Demanding my soul, my life, my all

NEVER LATE

He is never late, so learn to wait
On that important date for His name's sake

ODE TO THE GREAT I AM

Son of thunder, Elijah, prepares and drapes his mantle on his successor, Elisha, who continues to deal with age old sins – pride, idolatry, and willful disobedience. Indeed, there is nothing new under the sun! All the while, Israel's historical destiny is being wrapped in the perfect guidance of an omniscient, omnipotent God who rules steadily with His Sovereign purposes to ultimately show forth His power and glorious proof that He alone is God, and there is NO other. In spite of today's political instability, economic insolvency and religious apostasy, Israel's welfare, and ours, depend on faithful submission and total reliance on our covenant keeping King of Kings and Lord of Lords. To Him be all the praise forever and ever.

Amen and amen

OH COME

O come, oh come Immanuel
O come today
O come to stay
O come and be my every way

OUTPOURING

Oh Jesus, Oh Jesus
May I be an outpouring of YOUR Spirit this day
To some precious soul that may come my way

PRAYER I

Lord God, we can't possibly learn and have true
happiness until we come face to face with Thee.
Break us down until everything that blocks and keeps
us from the fullness of Thee is removed. Help us to be
so sick of self that we die at Thy cross. We know that we
can't live fully until we are emptied of all self.
Then may we come saying, "Lord, here I am; use
me as Thou dost see fit until I am fit for Thee
in Thy heavenly abode."

PRAYER II

O Lord, we know that all desires and thirst and
hunger pangs are precious gifts from Thee.
May we always thirst until we drink more deeply at
Thy well of living waters.
May we feast only on manna from Heaven until
our lives are transformed by Thy precious blood.
May we radiate and touch lives of others,
because they know that we know Thee in full
power as given by the Holy Spirit

PRAYER III

O Lord, our true and risen Lord, in Whom we move and have our reason for living, thanks be to Thee for all manifestations Thou has poured upon us. Most of all, thanks be to Thee for the blessed Person of Jesus Christ who speaks, directs, and permeates our innermost spirits until we can walk in the knowledge of Thy truth and life.

Amen

PRECIOUS LORD

Precious Lord, make me aware
with zealous love and jealous care
of all YOUR children everywhere.
Boldly to proclaim YOUR WORD, so it can be heard
and never thought absurd,
for YOUR truth triumphs over wrong
giving your servant a new song.

SALVATION'S PLAN

Mighty deliverer
Mighty God
Holy is YOUR NAME, for
Your love that stays the same

YOU engage us with YOUR plan
And hold us in YOUR mighty right hand,
So we are equipped to stand,
As we journey through this land
Spreading salvation's plan
Blessed be the LORD

Psalm 109:21

TEACH US LORD

O God, how our souls do ache and pain when we
see Thy children wandering and straying so far from Thee.
Teach us, Lord, that we may teach. Love us more
that we can give love even to our enemies.
Show us where and what to do that it can be done
to Thy honor and glory.

THANKS BE TO THEE

Thanks be to Thee,
The One in Three,
And have our being;
On Whom we do all our leaning,
If we're to go winging
Into Thy world as
Instruments for Thee!

THE LORD IS ALWAYS NEAR

Bless, seek, fear
For the Lord is always near.

Trust in Him above all,
For without Him you will fall.

So exalt His holy name,
For He remains the same.

Angels He sends to protect,
So glorify the Lord and reflect.

For His mercies endure
That is for sure.

Psalm 34

THE POTTER

You are the potter Lord,
So I present the clay,
That you can mold and have YOUR way.
Let nothing prevent full sway
To ever thwart YOUR way

THE TRUE VINE

Holy Spirit, truth Divine,
Make us part of Thy true vine;
Prune and weed us from ourselves
Until total brokenness prevails.

Then, and only then, dear Lord,
Can we find the golden cord
Which binds and roots us in Thy love
Until You come from above
To pick us from our earthly bower.

WISE FEAR

Bless, seek, fear, trust. In Christ, for this is a must!
Our refuge, shield and strength…there is simply no
    measurable length.

The more I taste and see, the more dear He becomes to me.

He is near in all distress and redeems so I can rest.

Yes, magnify the Lord our God so HE does not have
to apply the rod!

O bless the Lord, and all that's within me, bless His Holy Name
Who forever remains the same—my Jesus without shame.

Psalm 34
Proverbs 9:10

ZEALOUS LOVE

Lukewarm Christians not for me,
Because my Lord demands from me
Zealous love and jealous care
Of all His children everywhere.
God's not dead; we are dead instead,
Lost in trespasses and sin;
Open our eyes – unstop our ears
Until our hardened hearts do bend,
Proving Thou hast bled and shed
Tears of perfect love for us.

Profits from this book's sales go to support SAFE HARBOR in Hickory, North Carolina.

Vision Statement
To inspire everyone we encounter to a thriving and purposeful life in Christ.

Mission Statement
A Christ-centered community for rebuilding, renewing and recovery

Core Values
Integrity, Compassion, Humility, Collaboration, and Empowerment

See all we do at safeharbor.org

Scan the code above with your Smart Phone to visit our site.

Text to Give: Harbor @ 56512

ABOUT THE AUTHOR

Barbara C. Weathers was born and grew up in Winston-Salem, NC, having graduated from Reynolds High School in 1954 and four years later from Queens University in Charlotte, NC, with a BA degree in English. She was married two weeks following graduation to lawyer Carroll Weathers Jr., and was married 49 years. Six years later, in 1964, they moved from Wilson and Manteo to Hickory with their first child, Wayland. God chose to bless them with a second son, Charles, in March of 1965. After Wayland's death in 1970, The Lord added two more blessings: a third son, Harrison, and a precious daughter, Grace.

Barbara taught at St. Stephen's Elementary and Startown Schools in Catawba County, was once chosen Teacher of the Year, and also was given the *Siecor Outstanding Math-Science Teacher Award* in May, 1997.

Barbara has taught Sunday School, and until recently, sang in church choirs since third grade, tutored students in reading and math, and was a former member of The Hickory Choral Society and the Hickory Service League. She now loves living in Blowing Rock for half of the year, holding Grandbunny Camp, entertaining, writing, and studying the WORD. She also enjoys attending Bible Studies with Gena Welch Small as leader, reading, and cooking meals for friends with medical or celebratory reasons. She has an active prayer ministry, and sincerely hopes that *Legacy of Faith* will draw many to have a closer relationship with the Lord and will help all look forward to His glorious return.

Limited time special acrostic poem written by Barbara C. Weathers for this edition!

Please remove and share to support the people of Ukraine.

UKRAINE

Ukraine, mission-minded country

Keenly strong and bold in loving unity

Rigorous in righteous standing

A bulwark never-failing

Inspired and filled with loving purpose

Never to desert and give over their freedom rights

Engaged with endeavor to push through all obstacles, so as to withstand all fiery darts in Jesus' Name

Amen

Ephesians 6:16